Original title:
Purpose: Still a Work in Progress

Copyright © 2025 Creative Arts Management OÜ
All rights reserved.

Author: Lila Davenport
ISBN HARDBACK: 978-1-80566-262-4
ISBN PAPERBACK: 978-1-80566-557-1

A Quilt of Unwritten Chapters

Each patch on my quilt tells a tale,
Of coffee spills and a curious snail.
Sewing dreams with mismatched thread,
My cat thinks it's her royal bed.

Inspiration strikes with a sudden dance,
As I juggle plans in a comical trance.
Potholders and socks, a whimsical mess,
Who knew crafting could be such a stress?

The Unfinished Symphony

I conducted a band of breakfast treats,
With pancakes and syrup, oh what feats!
But the eggs rebelled, they scrambled instead,
Now my masterpiece sits, unbuttered, cold bread.

The audience left with their forks in dismay,
As my kazoo solo went wildly astray.
A symphony garbled, a high-pitched meep,
The final encore? Just a long, loud beep.

Resonance of Unspoken Hopes

My dreams hover near like a mirage,
Invisible plans in an unkempt collage.
I whisper to stars in the dead of night,
But they laugh and flicker, oh what a sight!

A wish on a comet, just out of reach,
I'll settle for pizza and a good beach.
With every slice, I forget my plight,
Hopes wrapped in cheese, a savory flight.

Mapping the Heart's Desires

I drew a map on the back of a napkin,
With arrows and doodles, what a fine caption!
To find my way, I got lost in the sauce,
Now the treasure's a buffet, oh what a gloss!

With each accidental heart-shaped cookie,
I realized my quests are far from spooky.
A compass that points to jellybeans sweet,
Who knew my desires would end up to eat?

Maps Marked with Uncertainty

With maps in hand, I set to roam,
But where I'm going? I still don't know!
My GPS keeps saying, 'Turn around!'
While I just smile, lost in this town.

I bought a guide to help me see,
But it pointed left, and I went right, you see.
I waved to a tree, thought it was a man,
Guess you could say my plan's on a span!

Seasons of Growth and Change

Springtime blooms and summer's sun,
Fall brings jackets, winter's fun!
I've tried yoga, and meditation too,
Yet here I am, still in my shoe.

Each season wears a different hat,
In winter, I wore my cozy cat.
So here's to growth, and a laugh or two,
For change is just glue that won't stick to you!

The Horizon's Relentless Call

The horizon laughs with a cheeky grin,
It I beckons close, yet pulls me again.
I pack a suitcase filled with dreams,
Then trip on the laces of my own schemes.

Chasing sunsets like a kid with a kite,
While the wind says, 'Wait, is that left or right?'
With every step I'm two steps behind,
But oh, what a frolic in whimsy I find!

Rewriting My Story with Each Breath

I hold my pen to rewrite the day,
'Hiccups are hurdles' is what I'll say!
Each word I scribble feels clumsy and bold,
Yet each line tells of adventures untold.

With every breath, a new plot twist,
Like losing my keys; 'Is that in the mist?'
I chuckle at life's little quirks and bends,
For every page turned, a new laugh descends!

Rays Breaking Through the Clouds

A penguin in a tuxedo, looking quite slick,
Wonders if he could complete a magic trick.
He flaps his flippers, gives it a try,
But all he produces is a blue fish pie!

The sun peeks out, gives a little cheer,
As the clouds conspire, 'Hey, let's disappear!'
With laughter and sunlight, they decide to play,
The penguin holds his fish, 'Well, that's my day!'

The Quest for Unwritten Chapters.

With a notepad full of doodles, the hippo said,
"Adventure's calling, but so is my bed!"
He donned a cape, made from bedsheet scraps,
And launched from the sofa, avoiding the naps!

A squirrel took notice, with a twitch of his tail,
"You can't fly too high; you might end up in jail!"
But the hippo was brave, with a belly so round,
He landed in cupcakes, now that's adventure found!

A Journey Yet Unfolded

On a road less traveled, a goat wore a hat,
"This feels quite fancy, but what of the cat?"
He daydreamed a plan, to host a grand ball,
But forgot to invite the big dog down the hall!

As the parrot squawked, 'What's the theme going to be?'
The goat pondered deeply, 'I'll just wait and see.'
With a hula-hoop there and some dance mats set right,
They vowed to make this the party of the night!

Threads of Becoming

In a cluttered room, a chameleon stood,
"Should I wear blue or a shade of good wood?"
As he twirled and twisted, colors did blend,
His outfit was busy; should've just gone with trend!

A rabbit hopped by, and gave him a glance,
"It's quite a bold choice for your next big dance!"
With a chuckle and flair, they took to the floor,
In threads of confusion, they found loads of more!

Notes in an Ongoing Symphony

I scribble notes in the dark,
Each one a missed cue, a lark.
The violin squeaks, the drum just fell,
Yet I dance still, casting my spell.

My conductor's a cat with a dream,
Purring along but missing the theme.
The melody wobbles like jelly on toast,
And still I sway, trying to coast.

The trumpet goes flat, the tuba's confused,
A symphony born of being bemused.
With laughter we play, a joyful spree,
In this concert of chaos, just let it be.

As we blend our sounds, it's a wild parade,
Not a masterpiece, but a grand charade.
Let's feign perfection while we misplay,
In this ongoing symphony, hooray, hooray!

Chasing Shadows of Meaning

I set off on a quest for the wise,
With a map that I drew—even I'm surprised.
The compass spins like it's lost its head,
Maybe I'll take a nap instead.

The shadow of thought plays peek-a-boo,
Whispers of wisdom, or maybe just stew?
I chase after ideas like cats chase tails,
Bumping into walls, and dodging the gales.

Each answer I find, just adds to the mess,
Like wearing a shirt that's too tight, I confess.
But giggles erupt when I trip on my dreams,
Life's not what it seems, or so it redeems.

So I wander through shadows, with glee in my stride,
As questions become friends, not something to hide.
I laugh at the riddles, a dance in the night,
Chasing these shadows, I'm feeling all right!

The Puzzle Yet to Be Solved

I open the box, pieces galore,
A thousand fragments scattered on the floor.
I twist and I turn, none seem to fit,
Is this a puzzle or a cosmic skit?

The corners are missing, and colors clash,
With each wrong try, I let out a laugh.
A dog steals a piece, thinking it's food,
Now I'm left with a wild attitude.

My friends cheer me on, offering aid,
But their advice gets tangled, with choices made.
We fit in some pieces, then shake our heads,
Is it art, is it chaos, or are we all neds?

At last, I surrender, give up the fight,
Accepting my puzzle is hopeless, all right.
With a chuckle and grin, I toss it away,
For life's not a puzzle, it's a playful display!

Diary of a Half-Formed Vision

Dear Diary, today I had a bright thought,
It vanished like socks—how do they get caught?
My mind's a sketchbook, half-drawn and undone,
A masterpiece waiting, or just lots of fun.

I woke up this morning, felt bold and inspired,
But the coffee kicked in, and my vision retired.
I scribble my dreams, but they wiggle and splat,
Like a dog handing over a random old hat.

Each entry's a trip, where logic takes flight,
With sentences zigzagging left and right.
I ponder my goals like they are jelly beans,
Sweet but wobbly, with no clear means.

So here's to the visions, both hazy and bright,
To the laughter we find in the midst of the plight.
In this diary's pages, I'll scribble and play,
For each quirk of my mind makes for a funny day!

The Bloom Before the Harvest

In a garden of dreams, I plant my thoughts,
Watering whims, some turn to knots.
With sunshine of laughter, and shadows of doubt,
I wait for the flowers to figure it out.

The bees buzz around, they have no clue,
Pollinating chaos in shades of blue.
I trip on a weed, oh what a surprise!
Who knew that these seeds had such wild alibis?

A sunflower dances, a daisy rolls eyes,
While I search for answers, the robin just sighs.
With quirky ambitions and catalogs of cheer,
I embrace the absurd, that's my career!

So here in my patch, a baffling sight,
I laugh at the plans that ran out of light.
The bloom still awaits, but here's the twist,
Each petal's a punchline I can't resist!

The Journey of the Incomplete

Footprints in sand, lead me astray,
With plans on a map and a mind in disarray.
I packed all the snacks, forgot the route,
But hey, every misstep adds flavor to the route!

A signpost that wobbles, it points to the moon,
While I chase down rainbows wearing a tuna costume.
My compass spins wild, but so does my grin,
Wandering in circles, that's where I begin.

A journey less perfect, more a stand-up show,
With punchlines that flourish wherever I go.
Misadventures make great stories to tell,
As I fumble and tumble through this whimsical spell.

So pass me the laughter, the quirks, and the glee,
In this puzzle I'm piecing, I find bits of me.
The incomplete saga is simply divine,
Just a dash of confusion, and everything's fine!

Traces of Tomorrow's Light

Stumbling through today, with yesterday's shoes,
Each step is a giggle, oh how I amuse!
The sunlight dances, mocking my stride,
While I trip over shadows that giggle and hide.

They say tomorrow's bright, but I lost that map,
Navigating life like I'm in a rap.
With rhymes that don't rhyme and lines that make sense,
I'm crafting tomorrow with paper and suspense.

A disco ball gleams from the edge of my dreams,
With sparkles of wisdom and hiccups of schemes.
Each plan falls apart, oh what a delight!
As I chase the shimmer of tomorrow's light.

So here's to the future, a wild, fuzzy bite,
Where laughter and life weave wrongs into right.
With traces of joy that bubble and blend,
I'll dance with uncertainty, my ever-lovely friend!

The Forge of Uncertainties

In a workshop of chaos, I hammer away,
Bending my dreams like clay in a play.
With a sprinkle of joy and an ounce of mishap,
Each ding on the anvil's a reason to clap.

The tools are all mismatched, the blueprint a mess,
But I grin at the chaos, no time to stress.
A wrench for a spatula, a saw for a pen,
I craft the uncharted with giggles and zen.

Oh, the projects are wild, the deadlines are late,
But who's really counting? It's all first-rate!
With sparks of confusion lighting up my face,
I'll forge through the muddle with style and grace.

So here in this furnace of whimsy and chance,
I shape my tomorrow with a happy dance.
Uncertainties glimmer like stars in the night,
As I laugh through the mess, it all feels just right!

The Tenderness of Trials

I tried to bake a cake today,
But all I got was goo.
Whisking dreams and flour dust,
Next time, I'll make it stew.

With every slip and slide I take,
There's laughter in the air.
It's not a failure, it's a quirk,
Life's comedy we share.

I brush my teeth while in a rush,
To toothpaste's daring flight.
It's all a part of growing up,
At least my smile's bright!

So here's to all the stumbles made,
And silly things we do.
Each blunder paints a brighter hue,
In this wild life's view.

A Bloom Amongst the Weeds

In a garden bold and bright,
A flower grew askew.
Surrounded by the prickly thorns,
With a grin, it just blew.

"I'm not quite perfect," it declared,
"Nor am I in my prime.
But who needs norms and rigid lines,
When life's a bowl of limes?"

Bees buzzed by with curious glee,
"Your petals are a sight!"
So what if I'm a little quirky?
I'm still a pure delight.

The daisies rolled their eyes at me,
As I danced in the breeze.
But I'm just here to soak up sun,
And spread a little tease.

Horizons Still Unwritten

I woke up with a grand plan,
To conquer all today.
But the cat had other options,
And curled up right away.

I set my sights on distant shores,
But found a couch instead.
Adventure can be tricky, see?
Especially when you're fed.

So, here I sit with cozy snacks,
And a good show to binge.
Life's not all about the grind,
Sometimes, you just cringe.

With a notebook full of dreams untold,
And popcorn in a heap,
I learn that every tiny change,
Is worthy of a leap.

The Tapestry of Untamed Thoughts

My thoughts are like a playful breeze,
    They swirl and prance around.
One minute I'm doing laundry,
    Next, I'm lost and found!

I write down all my brilliant dreams,
    Then promptly lose the pen.
I chase a thought like a wild hare,
    And feel like I'm ten again!

    Kites tangled in a treetop high,
    Fluffy clouds chasing sun.
    In this chaotic, blissful mess,
    Who say's I'm not much fun?

So here's to wild, untamed ideas,
    Let's dance in our own style.
For every twist and turn we take,
    We'll end with a big smile.

The Palette of Infinite Possibilities

Colors clash and collide,
A canvas quite absurd,
I'm painting with my left hand,
Expectations all unheard.

Dancing dots and splashes,
I laugh, then start anew,
What's blue? What's green? Who cares?
It seems I've lost my cue.

With brushes made of spaghetti,
And paint that tastes like cheese,
I find my way in chaos,
Embracing all with ease.

So paint another picture,
Or toss it in the air,
Each stroke a little giggle,
A masterpiece, if I dare.

The Soundtrack of Bold Beginnings

Blasting tunes from cans and pots,
With spoons as big as me,
I'm conducting my own symphony,
A chaotic jubilee.

Oh, every note's a tumble,
A cacophonous delight,
When trying to be serious,
I accidentally take flight.

There's rhythm in my stumbles,
As I step on a cat or two,
Each purr a note in harmony,
In this orchestra of goo.

So I hum and dance around,
Imagining a band,
With mismatched socks and laughter,
Together we all stand.

A Symphony Yet to Compose

A melody's a tricky beast,
It plays hide and seek,
I scribble on napkins and crumbs,
What's probably pure cheek.

With kazoo as my main instrument,
And maracas made of rice,
I compose with simple nonsense,
Rolling dice sounds so nice.

Each note is just a guesswork,
Each beat a playful dare,
I'll launch a playful symphony,
Though no one really cares.

But music fills the corners,
Of this cluttered little room,
Where laughter leads the chorus,
And silliness will bloom.

The Underbelly of Changing Seasons

Leaves are falling in my hair,
I'm dressed for winter's chill,
But summer's still in my headspace,
With ice cream dreams to fill.

Wearing shorts in autumn's breeze,
While sipping on hot tea,
I trip on falling acorns,
And giggle with pure glee.

Spring shows up with flowers,
That tickle at my nose,
While winter schemes and plots,
To douse me with snow and woes.

The seasons keep on changing,
While I just sit and sway,
In mismatched socks, I revel,
In this colorful ballet.

A Palette of Untouched Colors

In a world that's full of paint,
I spilled my dreams without restraint.
The canvas mocks my clumsy touch,
My masterpiece? It's not that much.

Splatters here, drips over there,
I promise that I had a care.
With every color, hues collide,
My vision blur, my humor wide.

The easel groans beneath the weight,
Of dreams not shaped and plans not great.
But every brushstroke leads to fun,
In this wild art, I'm still not done.

So laugh with me at my missed aim,
Creating joy is half the game.
Each canvas holds a chuckle dear,
In colors bright, my path is clear.

Echoes of That Which Is Yet to Be

In a room of echoes, voices shout,
'Take a leap!', they tease, no doubt.
Yet here I sit, in comfy socks,
Plotting dreams with my cereal box.

The clock ticks loud, it's past my time,
I sip my tea and think sublime.
What might I be, or hope to try?
A jester's heart or the next wise guy?

Ideas swirl, a dizzy dance,
Am I the lead or just a chance?
With laughter loud, I follow fate,
While tangled thoughts just wait and wait.

Yet in this ruckus, sparks ignite,
With giggles bright, my soul takes flight.
The future winks, a grin so wide,
For every stumble, there's joy beside.

The Heart of a Craft Still Molding

I knead my dreams like silly dough,
With flour fights and giggles flow.
Each shape I form is kind of neat,
Yet none quite match my messy beat.

The potter's wheel spins round and round,
While visions yet remain unfound.
A wobbly vase or funky bowl,
Each creation reflects my soul.

Lopsided mugs and crooked plates,
With every flop, my spirit skates.
On this craft path, I grin so wide,
For every goof, there's joy to ride.

So let me mold, and laugh a lot,
With every try, I find my spot.
In sculpted dreams, I'll twist and turn,
Just crafting laughs, it's my concern.

Glimmers in the Future's Veil

Peeking through a curtain thin,
I see bright flashes, grins, and spins.
The future's sharp, a little sly,
With silly hats and reasons why.

I tiptoe softly, not to scare,
The dreams that bounce with lively flair.
They whisper tales, a bit absurd,
Of clumsy jumps and laughs unheard.

With every giggle, hope grows strong,
In wobbly steps, I can't go wrong.
So I'll chase shadows, chase the light,
In this merry mix, my heart takes flight.

For in the veil of what may be,
Lies laughter loud and joy so free.
This journey's wild, but I must say,
I wouldn't have it any other way.

Unraveling the Canvas of Life

Life's a canvas, paint it bright,
Yet I spilled coffee, what a sight!
Colors mix, oh what a mess,
But who needs clean? I like the stress.

Every stroke, a wobbly dance,
Sometimes I trip, but it's my chance!
To add some green, or maybe red,
A masterpiece or just misread?

Scribbles here, and doodles there,
An artist's heart, but lacking flair.
Yet laughter's gold, my brush in hand,
Creating chaos, isn't it grand?

So here's my art, a winking grin,
With every flaw, a little win!
A gallery of joy and tease,
In this wild ride, I do as I please.

Embracing the Unknown

What's around the bend? A curious quest,
Maybe a monster, or just a jest?
With socks mismatched, I charge ahead,
Who knew "unknown" could fill with dread?

I tripped on dreams and fell on fears,
Danced with doubt while eating pears.
Each twisty turn, a laugh we chase,
Wearing life's confusing face.

Maps are silly, can't count on fate,
For every plan, there's more to grate.
A compass spins, like my old brain,
Trusting instincts, let's go insane!

So let's embrace the weird and wild,
Life's more fun when you're a child.
With open arms, I leap with glee,
The unknown's my favorite cup of tea!

Sketches of a Brightening Path

Sketches in my mind, not on the page,
Erasers gone, oh what a stage!
Doodling life, with crayons bright,
Like drawing cats that take to flight.

Each little sketch, a wild surprise,
Sometimes a bird, with butterfly eyes.
But when it falters, and starts to fade,
I just add glitter, and honey lemonade!

Pathway zigzags, it often bends,
Where does it lead? No one pretends.
With laughter loud, I trip and slide,
Embracing every twist, I ride!

So hand me joy, and let me scribble,
This life's a dance, no time to nibble.
With colors bright and grins unmasked,
I sketch a path, too fun to task!

The Rhythm of Evolutions

Life's a beat, can you feel the sway?
Sometimes it's jazz, others are bays.
I trip on toes, yet find the groove,
With every stutter, I'll make you move.

Evolution's song, a silly tune,
Swapping my hat like changing the moon.
From clumsy steps to a flair of grace,
Dancing with laughter, at my own pace.

Twists and turns, a funny ballet,
Juggling dreams while they drift away.
But with each spin, I find my place,
In this grand jive, there's no disgrace.

So let's keep dancing, no end in sight,
With giggles and grins, we'll shine so bright.
For life's a rhythm, we can't control,
But together in steps, we find our role!

Journeying Through Unfinished Dreams

I packed my bags and hit the road,
With lofty thoughts and a fearsome load.
But every map has a missing piece,
I ended up lost, oh what a feast!

Each detour adds a new design,
Like mismatched socks, they intertwine.
I stumble forth, with laughter and glee,
My journey's a mess, but it's home to me.

In search of gold at every corner,
I found my lunch; what a delight, I ponder!
Forget the goals, I'll roam and play,
In this wild maze, I'll spend my day.

So here's to dreams that roll around,
To joy in the chaos that can be found.
With each misstep, a chuckle's burst,
Life's greatest joy is to quench that thirst!

The Canvas of Tomorrow

I took my brush and made a mess,
Splatters of hope in the great express.
Colors ran wild, like kids at play,
Tomorrow's canvas? Who needs a sketch anyway!

I tried to paint my grand design,
But ended up with something divine.
Abstract art, a splash of cheer,
My masterpiece grows, year after year.

Each dab of paint a quirk, a laugh,
Turns out I'm great at the silly path.
Just let it flow, let colors blend,
Who knew the chaos could still transcend?

In this gallery of dreams awry,
Framed by laughter, I aim for the sky.
With every stroke, a tale retold,
In the canvas of life, my heart's pure gold!

Threads of Ambition Unraveled

I wove a tapestry of grand delight,
With threads of ambition that took flight.
But lo and behold, a knot appeared,
My vision's quite fuzzy, it's rather weird!

I tugged and pulled, trying to mend,
But each loop just seemed to twist and bend.
Like spaghetti on a plate, it's true,
My plans entangled, what to do?

Yet laughter came, I must confess,
I wore my chaos like a dress.
Who needs a plan? Let's dance, I say,
With threads unraveled, I'll find my way!

Each fiber tells a tale of jest,
A life that's crazy, but feels the best.
In this fabric, I'll stitch some cheer,
For every loop missed, there's joy right here!

In Search of My North Star

I charted the sky with a coffee mug,
Searching for answers in the morning tug.
Each star a goal, shining bright,
Yet I wandered off, lost in the nightlife!

I followed a squirrel, quite a surprise,
Thinking it knew where the treasure lies.
But instead of gold, I found a nut,
With laughter bubbling, I smiled and tut.

Tomorrow I'll navigate with glee,
A compass crafted out of whimsy.
Forget the map, let's dance instead,
With stars above, my troubles shred.

In search of a guide that knows the call,
I realized I'm content with it all.
So here's to stars, both near and far,
With joy in the journey, I'm my own star!

An Odyssey of Unwritten Tales

In a land where socks get lost,
The hero starts to weigh the cost.
With mismatched shoes and tangled hair,
He shuffles on without a care.

A sandwich stuck in yesterday's dream,
He wonders if it's more than it seems.
With every step, a jest awaits,
While time eludes him, life creates.

With catapulted socks on a quest,
He finds the humor in all the mess.
For laughter dances in every strife,
As he embarks on this silly life.

The tales unwritten, the laughs untold,
Between bites of pizza, dreams unfold.
An odyssey of quirks, laughter leads,
In this grand adventure, joy proceeds.

The Unraveled Thread of Thought

A spiral notepad, a jumbled mix,
Thoughts unspool like oddball tricks.
With silly doodles and cross-eyed sighs,
He writes with fervor, then loses the ties.

The cat walks by, a meow for his muse,
Disrupting the topic he'd gladly peruse.
A noodle strewn across the floor,
Becomes an idea, but leads to much more.

With every thought, a pithy quirk,
Jumping in circles like a playful jerk.
He stitches humor into each line,
Crafting a tapestry, one misstep at a time.

A web of laughs, mishaps galore,
In the unraveling, he finds his core.
With random epiphanies and laughable dread,
He learns that sometimes, just be led.

Illuminating the Shadows Ahead

With a flashlight that flickers, he starts his quest,
Exploring the corners where odd things rest.
Chasing reflections and shadows so eerie,
He bumps into walls, yet feels all cheery.

A banana peel's laugh echoes in air,
As he slips and he slides, without a care.
Each tumble and turn, a giddy delight,
In the shadowy dance of the unplanned flight.

With a map made of pizza stains and cheer,
He navigates life with laughter, sincere.
Illuminating the dusky unknown,
He finds that the heart deems every misstep home.

Through whispers of chaos and giggles he wades,
A silly explorer in life's endless charades.
Shadows may linger, but giggles will spread,
As he sheds light on what's ahead, full led.

Finding the Calm in the Storm

In the midst of chaos, where winds start to roar,
He brewed a storm tea more than folklore.
With tiny umbrellas and laughter so rolly,
He found peace in splashes, how quite jolly!

The raindrops tap-dance on the gutter's brims,
While he twirls his worries on whimsy's whims.
A rubber duck floats by, in a regal display,
As he navigates puddles, come what may.

Amidst the dark clouds, a bright sun peeks through,
He chuckles aloud at life's teasing view.
For thunder may rumble, and lightning may strike,
But he finds joy in the storms that hike.

So he sails on splashes, a captain so brave,
Amidst all the frenzy, he learns how to save,
A laugh here and there, a giggle will form,
In each little tempest, he finds the warm.

Flickers of a Forthcoming Flame

The candle wobbles, what's the aim?
Hot wax drips like life's odd game,
My ideas dance, a jumbled cheer,
But in the chaos, joy is near.

A spark ignites, then fizzles fast,
Like my plans for a bright forecast,
I scribble notes with a crayon pen,
And wonder if I'll start again.

In the chaos, a laugh I find,
As unplanned moments unwind,
Each little mishap, a tale to tell,
It's a riot, oh can't you tell?

With every stumble, I take a leap,
Creating mischief, my heart to keep,
So let the clumsy moments rise,
For in the flops, the laughter lies.

Paved with Half-Built Bridges

A bridge I built with popsicle sticks,
Each time I try, it end in tricks,
Halfway done, it starts to sway,
Will it hold? Who's to say?

Here's a plan, oh what a dream,
But then I trip on my own scheme,
Ropes of laughter swing so wide,
As I contemplate this wild ride.

Steps ahead, yet steps behind,
Yet joy is found within the grind,
I'll hop along these quirky paths,
Amidst the giggles and the gaffes.

A blueprint tossed, the paint still wet,
Yet I look back—no regrets just yet,
For every draft that falls apart,
Brings laughter close, a work of art.

Stitching Together Possibilities

With thread too short, I take a chance,
Sewing dreams, a wobbly dance,
Each stitch a laugh, each knot a grin,
In this fabric, I dive in.

Cloth of sunlight, patch of gloom,
I twirl and spin in this small room,
A quilt of wishes, wrinkled seams,
But who needs neat in silly dreams?

I pull and tug, the fabric frays,
Yet I am here to weave the play,
Laughter blooms in every fold,
In every color, stories told.

So gather round, embrace the mess,
A masterpiece in goofy dress,
Each thread a laugh, a joyful thread,
In this fabric dance, let's be led.

Through the Cracks of Routine

Each morning greets me with a yawn,
Like a cat, half awake, I'm drawn,
To coffee spills and breakfast slime,
Creating chaos feels like rhyme.

I schedule fun but lose the beat,
While errands dance on little feet,
Routine has cracks like chips in glass,
But through them, goofy moments pass.

I juggle tasks with humor bright,
In the mayhem, I find my light,
A twist of fate, or slapstick laugh,
Turns everyday into a giffy math.

So here's to life, a twisty road,
With ups and downs, and giggles owed,
Through cracks of order, joy will peek,
In every blunder, life's unique.

Dreamcatcher of Future's Call

I caught a dream inside a net,
It wriggled free, I must confess.
With every twist, it made a bet,
Said, "Life's a game, so don't digress!"

I chased it down, it tossed and spun,
Wore mismatched socks, my hair a mess.
Each step I took, let's call it fun,
But all I found was last week's press!

The future's bright, or so they say,
But my compass points to nowhere fast.
I dance around like it's ballet,
And laugh aloud at the questions cast!

So here I stand, a joker's role,
With dreams in tow, I wave my wand.
Each giggle hints at my true goal,
To catch a laugh, and then respond!

Beneath the Surface of Now

I paddle hard in murky streams,
Digging deep for what I need.
But all I find are twisted dreams,
Like socks and toys—what a strange breed!

The water swirls with silly thoughts,
A fish that talks, a bridge that sings.
I ponder if my mind just rots,
Or if this is what living brings.

The rocks are wise, but play the fool,
With grins that dare me to explore.
Am I too close to nature's pool,
Or do they just want me to snore?

Among the weeds, I laugh and slip,
With giggling frogs as my best pals.
In laughter's grip, I take a dip,
And ponder life's odd, wiggly pals!

The Eclipse of Certainty

A shadow looms, my mind sets sail,
Certainties fade, they jiggle and jerk.
I search for answers, but it's a tale,
Of mismatched shoes and a cheeky smirk.

No path in sight, just clouds above,
Decisions bounce like bouncy balls.
I think I'm wise, but here's the shove:
It's me who's peeking through the walls!

Eclipsed by doubts, my thoughts take flight,
While random whims perform a dance.
I giggle at the strange delight,
Of catching chance in a silly trance.

So here I am, a cosmic joke,
With stars that laugh at my misstep.
In shadows deep, I light my smoke,
And toast to dreams that haven't crept!

Melodies of the Unvoiced

In silence hums a cheeky tune,
A chorus of the half-spoken words.
I tap my feet, I sway like a loon,
With melodies floating like silly birds.

They whisper doubts, but I just laugh,
For music plays where voices shun.
I'll dance my jig on life's old path,
While hidden notes forget to run.

A tune's a spark, a rhythm shared,
Of crazy quirks and grinning faces.
I stumble forth, unprepared,
But here we are, in cozy places.

With beats that skip and hops that fling,
I gather all the dreams I find.
In laughter's arms, I take to wing,
And let the melodies unwind!

Sculpting Tomorrow's Echo

With chunks of clay and dreams in hand,
We shape with laughter, not just planned.
A nose that wobbles, eyes askew,
Artistry dancing—how about you?

Each curve a giggle, each line a jest,
We mold our futures, doing our best.
Yet when it falls, like my lunch today,
We just laugh louder and shout, 'Hooray!'

Chasing visions, we stumble and trip,
Creating masterpieces of our own script.
In this chaos, we find our beat,
Sculpting echo's rhythm, oh what a feat!

So roll the clay, let's make a mess,
Each flub a treasure, a badge to bless.
Tomorrow's calling us, come what may,
With giggles and grins, we'll find our way.

The Dance of Potential

Twirl and spin, oh what a sight!
With two left feet, we dance with fright.
Each misstep shouted like a cheer,
'Void of grace but full of cheer!'

Frogs in tuxedos leap around,
Seeking rhythm, where fun is found.
We shake our limbs in joyful clout,
Who knew ambition could be this stout?

Jiving through mischief, we trip and laugh,
Our aspirations, a wobbly craft.
'Just one more step!', but we crash and roll,
Laughing our way to a bright, warm goal.

So why not dance on this grand parade?
With glittered dreams that never fade,
Just look at us, each twirl and flee,
In the dance of hope, we're wild and free!

Seeds of Ambition

Plant a seed, watch it grow,
Water it with laughter, let it flow.
The fertilizer? Just silly puns,
Helping us bloom under shining suns.

Tangled roots in the garden bed,
Growing sideways, 'Hey, not my head!'
Each sprout a giggle, a playful shout,
"Oh look, my to-do list wore out!"

Digging deeper, we find the quirks,
Like socks with holes and silly smirks.
Yet in our hearts, ambition swells,
Beneath the surface, our humor dwells.

So scatter joy, let it take flight,
The garden of dreams will be just right.
For every seed, a hearty grin,
In the field of hope, we all can win!

Labyrinth of Aspirations

In a maze of wishes, we roam about,
Dodging walls of doubt and shout.
With giggles loud as we spin and twist,
Finding the path that feels like bliss.

Left or right? It's anyone's guess,
A hedge of aspirations and silly mess.
Each turn we take is met with glee,
Who knew getting lost could feel so free?

We run in circles, yes, it's a blast,
Collecting memories—outfits from the past.
With every corner, we seize the day,
In this labyrinth, we laugh and play.

So come to our riddle, don't hesitate,
Together we'll wander, we won't be late.
For through the twists, we'll find our way,
In our joyful quest, we're here to stay!

Whispers of a Future Yet to Come

In socks that mismatched dance with fate,
I trip over dreams, they don't cooperate.
Future's behind, waving 'hello',
Yet I stand still, tripping on toe.

With coffee grounds guiding my way,
I sprinkle plans like spices in play.
A map made of doodles, oh what a sight,
Where's the next stop? I'm still in mid-flight.

To-do lists grow legs and run for the hills,
While I chase after them with half-baked thrills.
Life's an odd jigsaw, pieces uncanned,
Maybe someday I'll understand.

But as I sip tea from a garden of quirks,
I'll dance with my doubts and laugh at the jerks.
With each silly fall, I might just uncover,
A version of me that I could discover.

Building Bridges in the Fog

I'm out here with planks, my hammer to swing,
Building a bridge while the clouds do cling.
Each nail's a question; the answers are shy,
But I'll keep on swinging, asking, and why?

Fog rolls in thick, like a shy little ghost,
Guess it doesn't know what I need it for most.
I yell out my thoughts, can you hear me now?
The fog just chuckles, no need to bow.

In this muddled maze, I trip on my dreams,
With visions of triumph and cocoa creams.
I build with laughter, a glue that's absurd,
As each whispered thought adds humor to curd.

Finally, a bridge that's wobbling too much,
But hey, it's my magic, my brilliant touch!
In the fog I find fun, and maybe some cheer,
Building a future, just still not quite clear.

The Light Beyond the Horizon

Chasing a light through the muddy oak grove,
Wearing mismatched shoes on this wild little trove.
The horizon whispers it's just over there,
But I'm stuck tripping on the knots in my hair.

With dreams made of pasta and sauce made of cheer,
I noodle around, but the exit's not near.
That light keeps on teasing, a glow and a flick,
Like a firefly zooming, but no, it's a trick.

I wave to the clouds, raise a mug full of foam,
"Hey future, come closer, or I'll need a new home!"
Yet each step feels right, even if I fall,
I'm dancing with light and I'm loving it all.

So what if my path is a soft squishy mess?
In this joyfully weird hunt, I truly feel blessed.
With a chuckle and grin, I'll keep reaching high,
For the light on the horizon, I'll give one more try.

Scribbles of a Seeking Heart

Crayons in hand, let the wild scribbles flow,
A seeking heart draws, but where does it go?
Lines twist and turn, like a wiggly worm,
Landing on paper, bringing life to each term.

In the chaos of color, confusion takes flight,
A rainbow of dreams, oh what a delight!
Every smudge and splash tells a wacky new tale,
As I color outside the lines without fail.

Thoughts zing like rubber bands ready to snap,
Chasing every whim, taking a quick lap.
With laughter I scribble, oh what a grand art,
Embracing the mess of my seeking heart.

In simple intentions, my joy finds a voice,
With crayons and giggles, I make a bold choice.
Though the lines may be crooked, the colors fly free,
I'll scribble my story, just wait and see.

Dreams on a Loom of Time

In the weave of day and night,
I stitch my hopes with peculiar thread,
Each loop a laugh, each knot a fight,
My fabric's a dance, not just a spread.

I planned to knit a sweater fine,
But got a scarf that's way too wide,
Still it keeps my heart aligned,
With each mistake, I wear it with pride.

A quilt of dreams, with patches bright,
I toss in snippets of my blunders,
They sparkle like glitter in the light,
A cozy comfort amid life's wonders.

So here I stand, with needles in hand,
In a workshop of laughter and cheer,
I may not craft a perfect strand,
But I'll keep creating year after year.

The Fable of an Unfinished Journey

Once there was a tortoise slow,
Who claimed to know the way ahead,
Each step a giggle, don't you know?
He tripped on daisies, laughed instead.

The hare darted by with great finesse,
But paused for snacks, a quick delight,
Their race a jest, a fun excess,
As laughter echoed through the night.

They both agreed to skip the end,
To chase a butterfly, quite a sight,
Their story's twists, around the bend,
Unraveled happiness with every flight.

So here's to journeys left halfway,
To paths with bumpy, silly turns,
In each misstep, we find our play,
And from these tales, a love still burns.

Fragments of a Soul's Quest

A puzzle pieced with missing bits,
I search for that one corner square,
  Each time I try, the chaos fits,
 Like socks that vanish into thin air.

 I hang my hopes on pegs of fate,
But find they often slip and slide,
With each new quest, I celebrate,
 The crazy ride, my spirit's guide.

Not every fragment finds its place,
  Some make a hat, others a shoe,
 Yet in this merry, wild embrace,
I find myself, both cracked and true.

So gather 'round, all lost and found,
   Join me in this quirky game,
  In every piece, a joy profound,
 Our brokenness can spark a flame.

The Alchemy of Potential

I mixed a potion with a dash of dreams,
A sprinkle of hopes, and giggles galore,
It bubbled over, bursting at the seams,
    Creating chaos that I can't ignore.

A wizard hat made from old sock threads,
With spells of comfort woven in the yarn,
Each wand I grab, unpredictably spreads,
    A flash of whimsy, an accidental charm.

I brewed some stories, stirred in a laugh,
The cauldron sparked with vibrant delight,
Though many tales went off the path,
    Even messiness can feel just right.

So here's to potions that never quite set,
To laughter's spark in a bubbling brew,
In alchemy's dance, there's no regret,
For even weak spells can shine anew.

The Echoes of What Could Be

In the kitchen, I tried to bake,
A soufflé that looked like a flake.
It wobbled and jiggled, oh what a sight,
My dreams of a chef? Not quite right.

I thought I could dance like a star,
But two left feet? That's who we are.
With each little twirl, I spin like a top,
My aspirations? They all flop.

I wanted to run like the wind in the breeze,
But my cardio's not fit for such feats with ease.
I jogged for a minute, then found a nice bench,
Turns out my goals need a good old quench.

So here I stand, a work of my own,
An artist in life, still overthrown.
With laughter and mishaps, I'll gently parade,
A carnival dreamer, unafraid to invade.

A Tapestry of Hopes and Trials

I aimed for the stars, but hit the ground,
In my quest for glory, I made quite a sound.
With dreams like balloons, I watched them all pop,
But here I am laughing, I won't ever stop.

I knitted my wishes with yarn full of cheer,
But chose a bright color that screams out of fear.
Now my sweater looks like a circus gone mad,
But wearing it out? Well, that's just my fad.

I penned down my thoughts, oh what a delight,
But my poetry skills vanished from sight.
Instead of deep prose, I got rhymes about cats,
A collection of giggles, and brimmed with spats.

So I weave my mishaps into a grand tale,
With threads of my laughter, I'll never go pale.
Each knot tells a story, and each twist is a cheer,
In this crazy tapestry, I'll hold my dreams near.

The Sculptor's Hands in Motion

With a chisel in hand, I aimed to create,
A masterpiece crafted with love and debate.
But my first block of stone looked quite perplexed,
A blob of confusion that left me vexed.

I sculpted a figure, or thought I had done,
But it looked like my cat, who stole all the fun.
With mounds of clay and a swirling spree,
I ended up making a weird fruit tree.

I tried to carve grace from a solid block,
But ended up with a weird, crooked clock.
Its hands spun around like they'd lost all their time,
A quirky reminder my art's not a crime.

So on I will go, with my tools in a mess,
Creating with laughter, I'll never feel stress.
My sculptures may wobble, but who needs the prize?
I'll form little giggles and watch dreams arise.

Steps on a Winding Path

I took a long stroll on a path all askew,
Expecting straight lines but found a zoo.
With each twist and turn, I tripped on a root,
My journey was wobbly, like a cow in a suit.

I thought I could sprint through life's little race,
But ended up walking at a turtle's pace.
With every small step, I learned something new,
That running in circles can be quite a view.

I packed up my troubles, weighed down by the load,
But dropped every burden down that winding road.
Now I'm free to explore, without worry or doubt,
Just a wanderer's giggle, seeing what it's about.

So off I will wander, on paths yet untold,
Finding joy in the curves, and the mighty unfold.
With laughter and play, I'll stay in the game,
For every misstep's a chapter, never the same.

Embracing Impermanence

Life's a dance on a wobbly floor,
Trying to find what we're here for.
With each misstep, we tousle our hair,
Laughing at fate, with all its odd flair.

Plan in one hand and chaos in tow,
Life's a buffet, and we just want to grow.
Rolling with punches, we laugh and we cry,
Waving goodbye as plans pass us by.

Stumbling through moments we thought we would cherish,
Collecting the snippets that sometimes embarrass.
In this circus that life tends to be,
We find our own way to dance wild and free.

So here's to the journey, a farcical ride,
Finding sweet joy in what's untried and untried.
Each twist and turn is a giggle to share,
As we spin through the air, without a single care.

A Path Woven by Courage

With every step, the shoes might squeak,
But we strut it out, even if we feel weak.
Stumbling through bumps that life does dispense,
Falling down hard, but laughing makes sense.

Each leap is a works-in-progress-to-make,
Like a cat on a roof, trying not to shake.
We climb with greatly misplaced precision,
Juggling our dreams with charming derision.

The mountain may crumble, or the bridge may sway,
Yet we leap like rabbits, hopping away.
Fueled by our blunders, we gleefully tread,
With courage as clumsy as our grand dreams ahead.

So here's to the bravado we fashion each day,
To the stories we'll tell in a roundabout way.
Life's a mad sketch, colored wildly with glee,
As we waddle, we giggle, forever carefree.

Building a Horizon of Dreams

With paintbrushes made of spaghetti strands,
We sketch out our hopes in odd, messy bands.
Each swirl and curve could resemble a mess,
Yet isn't that charm? It's our playful finesse!

We gather our thoughts like lost socks in pairs,
Piling them high as we climb up the stairs.
Our skyline a riddle of giggles and sighs,
Where ambition and foolishness whimsically ties.

We plant all our seeds in a garden of cheer,
Watered with coffee and just the right beer.
As we dance through our dreams, in mismatched socks,
Finding a rainbow in unyielding blocks.

So here's to the mess, the clutter we mend,
With laughter as glue on which we depend.
Each dream's a jest, a whimsical scheme,
Building a horizon that's bursting with dreams.

Fables of What Might Be

In the land of perhaps, with a wink and a grin,
We craft our tall tales, where do-overs begin.
Each 'what if' echoes from valleys of fun,
As we chase after rainbows that finish a pun.

The stories we weave can be splendidly strange,
A spaghetti monster with great plans to change.
With laughter our guide, and our hopes as balloons,
Navigating tides on an ocean of tunes.

We barter with fate over cups of hot tea,
What if the future's a big slice of glee?
We snag at the future, our dreams in a bag,
Turning simple days into a playful hag.

So here's to the fables, so wildly absurd,
To embrace the unknown, to leap without word.
With giggles our compass, destined to see,
What might just unfold in this grand jubilee.

Reflections in a Growing Pond

In the pond, the frogs declare,
Life's a joke, if you dare!
They leap and splash, a silly team,
Chasing dreams like ice cream.

The lilies float, with grace they spin,
Whispering tales of where they've been.
The dragonflies buzz, in skies they dart,
Laughing and playing, like a work of art.

A turtle plods with wisdom slow,
But in its heart, there's room to grow.
The fish swim by with a glimmering grin,
Sharing secrets, where to begin.

So here's to the pond, where all is bright,
Crafting new stories, day and night.
In a growing world, we trip and fall,
Learning to laugh through it all.

Dawning of the Unbecome

The sun creeps up with a yawning sigh,
Its rays tickle clouds in the sleepy sky.
Morning unfolds in a whimsical way,
As naps turn to giggles, oh, what a day!

An alarm clock rings, but I hit snooze,
Living my life in a playful cruise.
I stumble in slippers, still half asleep,
Finding new laughs in thoughts that I keep.

The coffee pot hisses, a bubbling friend,
Promising warmth as the odd dreams blend.
With every sip, I dance and sway,
Becoming someone in my own silly way.

So here's to becoming, however we may,
With laughter and fun along the way.
In the dawn of nonsense, let us greet,
Every twist and turn, oh, what a treat!

The Flame Beneath the Ashes

In the fireplace, embers cling tight,
A flicker sparks in the deepening night.
Once it roared, now it's just a glow,
Yet underneath, there's still a show!

The logs that fell, they thought they'd end,
But ashes tell tales that start to blend.
With a gentle poke, a laugh we find,
Remnants dance in the wisp of the mind.

Neighbors peek in, they want a seat,
To share the warmth, oh, isn't that sweet?
We roast our marshmallows and tell our tales,
As the silly wind plays its gusty gales.

So here's to the flame, though it may seem dead,
It flickers and fumbles, alive instead.
In the depths, it's a raucous party inside,
With laughter and joy, let's all take a ride!

A Story Still in Ink

With a pen in hand, I scribble and scrawl,
My pages are messy, but I'm having a ball.
Each line a chuckle, each word a cheer,
A tale of mischief that's perfectly unclear.

The characters wiggle, they wiggle and squirm,
With plots that twist and take a new turn.
There's a fish on the run, and a cat with a hat,
Creating a ruckus, oh where's it at?

With every eraser, I laugh and I sigh,
For perfection's a myth, let's give it a try.
Inky fingers, and ideas that flop,
Yet, somehow, they bubble, they bounce and they pop.

So here's to the ink, and the laughter it brings,
To stories that wobble on zany little wings.
With joy in the process, let's let it all flow,
For a tale that's a riot is a tale that we know!

Realigning the Compass of Soul

My compass spins a silly dance,
Caught between a whim and chance.
Directions listed in a jumbled mess,
I'm just trying to find some finesse.

A pirate's map, or so I thought,
Turns out, it was just a parking spot.
X marks the spot for lost car keys,
And a coffee break, if you please.

The needle points to what I crave,
Like that secret stash of buttery wave.
With every wrong turn, a giggle I share,
Life's a joyride; who says it's unfair?

I laugh as I fumble through each detour,
Finding treasure in missteps, that's for sure.
Each twist in the path becomes a delight,
In this wacky journey, I'm taking flight.

Beneath the Stars of Ambition

Under bright lights, I set my goals,
With the grace of a cat on a roll.
I shoot for the moon, trip on a shoe,
And dream of success in neon hues.

Stars twinkle above, giving me sass,
While I'm busy inventing a new kind of grass.
Maybe it's purple, or maybe it glows,
If this is a fail, it's all part of the show!

Late-night snacks fuel my lofty dreams,
As I ponder life's quirky schemes.
The cosmos chuckles, "What's that you said?"
I'll figure it out – right after this bread.

With each bite, I craft a grand plan,
Full of pizzazz, like an overcooked pan.
The chase is where laughter finds its home,
Just don't forget to bring your own comb!

The Sculptor's Unfinished Work

Chiseled lines in a block of stone,
A face emerges, but it's all alone.
A nose like a squirrel, with googly eyes,
I swear I'm a genius in disguise!

Tools scattered, oh what a mess,
I swear the marble's out to impress.
With every chip, another laugh blooms,
Only in here do chaos find rooms.

Art isn't finished, but it's got flair,
It hums a ditty, a jig in mid-air.
My masterpiece speaks in clumsy tones,
Funny how art just sticks to its bones.

So come witness my grand exhibition,
With floors littered from each wild mission.
Who needs refinement, polished or neat?
With a charming quirk, my work is complete!

Façades That Fade

I wear a mask at the masquerade,
Dancing along, oh what a charade!
Behind painted smiles and costumes grand,
Lies a truth that might just be unplanned.

In a world where perfection's all the rave,
I strut like a peacock, though I misbehave.
Falling flat in my sequined shoes,
Yet I still charm with my quirky views.

Each façade cracks like an overripe fruit,
Revealing joy in my mismatched suit.
Laughter echoes through this silly spree,
As I embrace the mess that is me.

So here's to the masks we've all adorned,
Each a tale, both hilarious and worn.
In each stumble, a giggle we find,
Let's celebrate the crazy, the one-of-a-kind!

The Art of Unfinished Dreams

In a room full of boxes, I look for my muse,
Where socks have their dance, and I'm nursing a bruise.
A canvas of chaos, paints splatter and spill,
Yet here in this mess, I can dream at my will.

With every new scribble, the plan starts to shift,
An idea takes shape, then it flicks like a gift.
I laugh at the sketches that lead me astray,
But they whisper, 'Dear friend, we'll get there someday!'

A half-finished pancake lies lonely and cold,
As I chase after visions that never grow old.
With flour on my face and my hair in a bun,
I'm painting my future, it's all just good fun.

So here's to the dreams that never quite end,
With giggles and hiccups, around every bend.
I'll gather my thoughts like a proud parade,
And dance with the tunes of the plans I have made.

In the Midst of Transformation

I woke up today with a plan to be great,
But coffee went flying, and I'm running late.
My calendar's chaos, it's full of old jokes,
Yet through all the madness, I'm laughing with folks.

With hair that's a fright and a wardrobe that's loud,
I step to the mirror, feeling oh so proud.
In my pajamas, I strut with a grin,
Declaring the title of 'Queen of the Sin!'

Each hiccup's a story, I cherish the chase,
For change isn't perfect, but oh, it's my pace.
I'm weaving my life like a patchwork of cheer,
Embracing the journey, my dreams brought near.

So cheers to the moments that never align,
For laughter in journey is simply divine.
I'll wobble and giggle, embrace every sway,
In this wild transformation, I'm here to stay!

Steps Toward the Horizon

With sneakers unmatched, I wander the streets,
Counting each step, while inventing new feats.
The horizon calls softly, a mirage in sight,
But I trip on my laces, oh what a delight!

I'll hop like a bunny, then walk like a crab,
Each twist and each turn, adds flair to the drab.
With a map full of doodles, I'm lost but I know,
These steps make the journey, so onward I go.

The sun sets behind me, turning rays into gold,
While my slightly loose shoes, make stories unfold.
"Where's your destination?" the wise ones will ask,
"To laughter and joy!" is my cryptic task.

With each merry misstep, I waltz to the beat,
The dance of my dreams has me shuffling my feet.
I'll clap for my stumbles, my giggles, my falls,
For steps toward the horizon are the best of all!

Chasing Shadows of Tomorrow

I ran after shadows that danced on the wall,
With giggles and squeaks, I was ready to sprawl.
"What do you chase?" asked a friend with a frown,
I answered, "The laughter that brings joy around!"

With pockets of sunshine and sprinkles of fears,
I'm juggling my hopes while I sip my cold beers.
The shadows keep darting, like pop-up ads gone mad,
Yet I giggle and skip, feeling better than bad.

A kite made of dreams, it soars on a string,
But tangling in branches, it makes my heart sing.
"To tomorrow!" I cheer with a wink and a hop,
For shadows can't catch me, I'll never stop!

So here's to the chase, and the giggles we find,
In the dance of the future, I'm unconfined.
With every wild thought, the horizon draws near,
Chasing those shadows makes my purpose clear!

Whispers of a Dreaming Heart

In the land of hopes and schemes,
I tripped over my own dreams.
A blueprint sketched with crayon bright,
Yet I still can't find my light.

Amidst the plans I tried to draft,
I wedged my foot in a big gaffe.
I swear I scribbled the right address,
But I wound up in the land of mess.

So here I am with hearts in tow,
Navigating paths I hardly know.
With every wrong turn, laughter's bait,
Turns out I'm still a work in fate.

But in this chaos, joy resides,
With every stumble, the spirit glides.
Chasing dreams like a puppy's chase,
Let's just enjoy the wacky race.

Navigating Uncertain Waters

Set sail on life's great sea,
With a map drawn in crayon, just for me.
The stars align, or so I thought,
But lost is really all I've got.

My compass spins, oh what a jest!
It said do east, but I head west.
Filled with snacks and a cheeky grin,
I laugh at the mess I'm in.

Fishes laugh as I float by,
While dolphins watch with a curious eye.
Splashing waves are my only crew,
Yet I'm still paddling, who knew?

With every wave, I learn and grow,
Sailing on with an unsure flow.
As long as there's wind and a good breeze,
I'll keep on trying, with silly ease.

Mosaic of Intentions

I've pieced a puzzle of grand design,
But the corners are missing—what a sign!
With tiles of dreams in shades so bright,
I'm still searching for the truth in sight.

My masterpiece is quite the sight,
A rainbow swirl of what feels right.
Yet every time I think I see,
I bump my head on creativity.

Glue it down, or let it rest?
Each fragment screams it's truly blessed.
But with such chaos, can it thrive?
I guess it's fun just to survive.

In this gallery of my making,
Each blunder feels like joy in baking.
So here's to the mess that makes me whole,
A mosaic, sure, but it's got soul!

Horizons Yet to Be Discovered

I gaze at horizons, wide and far,
Dreaming big under the morning star.
Yet each dawn brings a new delay,
I can't even find my way to play.

With a map that's clearly out of date,
I wander down paths that tempt my fate.
With every step, a silly blunder,
Life's a stage of zany wonder.

Over hills and silly dales,
I'll seek the truth through epic fails.
A treasure hunt with clues askew,
Yet joy's the gem I'm digging through.

In each misstep, a giggle grows,
Life's a riddle where laughter flows.
So here's to horizons, bright and tough,
I'll find my way, though it's all a bluff.

Picking up the Pieces of New Dreams

When dreams fall like puzzle bits,
I pick them up, I laugh, I quit.
With a twist and a turn, I retry,
Making magic from sparks that fly.

Scattered thoughts in a shopping cart,
Collecting wishes, a work of art.
I paint with colors, messy and bright,
Who knew chaos could be such delight?

A dream's like a sandwich, oh so stacked,
Sometimes it's mustard where joy is packed.
I nibble and chew, and sometimes I spit,
Finding flavor in all of it.

So here I am, with glue and glue,
Creating something that's oddly new.
With mismatched pieces, I'll call this mine,
Laughter echoes where chaos aligns.

Canvas of a Dreaming Soul

My canvas is splashed with paint blunders,
A collage of laughter, life, and blunders.
With brushes that dance and colors that scream,
I sketch the mishaps of this goofy dream.

Each stroke tells a tale; yes, it's true,
About how I tried but forgot my shoe.
A masterpiece crafted from tripping mistakes,
Art by an artist who giggles and shakes.

The paint drips down, a waterfall race,
Accidental splatters, a joyful embrace.
I step back and ponder, what do I see?
A portrait of chaos, oh fabulous me!

Brush in hand, I'm wild and free,
Creating my world, just let it be.
For each laugh and slip, I hold it tight,
In this clumsy dance, my heart takes flight.

The Quiver of Daring Hearts

In a world where arrows never fly straight,
We laugh and we trip, it's never too late.
Daring hearts don quivers of bold delight,
With every misfire, we scream with delight.

Aim for the moon, but hit the catwalk,
Falling with grace in our wobbly walk.
Each step's an adventure, a giggle parade,
To conquer the unknown, we're fearlessly made.

With every bold leap, we wobble and roll,
But hey, who knew blunders could spark the soul?
Together we dance on this crooked line,
In a tangle of joy, watch our hearts shine.

So here's to the daring, the clumsy, the brave,
We're champions of laughter, the joy that we crave.
With arrows that misfire but spirits that dart,
We'll chase after dreams with a jubilant heart.

Signposts Along the Way

I wander along this whimsical street,
Signposts waving, a funny retreat.
"Turn left for fails, veer right for glee,"
Navigating life with a chuckle and spree.

Each marker a giggle, each bend a surprise,
Who knew the route could open our eyes?
A detour to joy, with roadblocks of fun,
We laugh through the stops 'til the day is done.

With quirky directions that make no real sense,
I'll follow my heart; it's my best defense.
A compass of chuckles, as silly as can be,
I'm on a wild journey—come ride with me!

So here's to the signposts that lighten the load,
With laughter and joy on this curious road.
Let's frolic through life, each step a delight,
With signposts that guide us, and spirits so bright.

Blossoming Between the Lines

In a garden of thoughts, I plant my dreams,
But weeds show up, bursting at the seams.
A daisy claimed it's the best of the bunch,
While I wrestle with my morning crunch.

Sunshine tickles, rain gives a lift,
Yet why do my plants seem so adrift?
They all wave hi, but no one's in line,
Tangled in growth, but hey, I'm just fine!

Time ticks on in a dance of delight,
My buds laugh, "You've got your head in the light!"
Each crooked stem tells a story so bold,
Watch me bloom into chaos untold!

So here's to the mess and the mishaps in bloom,
Finding joy in the funky perfume.
In this patch, I'll toil, take a wild swing,
For laughter, I find, is the best sort of spring.

Paths Yet to Be Walked

I packed my bags with socks and bad puns,
A map that misleads and a couple of buns.
The road calls me with a whimsical shout,
"Are we there yet?" Oh, the fun is in doubt!

With a compass that only points towards snacks,
I'll wander these woods on my silly little tracks.
Every twist and turn leads to somewhere new,
But the squirrels keep laughing; what's wrong with my view?

Trip on a branch and fall on my face,
Is this the great journey or a foolish race?
I'll take sixty steps and of course, I'll trip,
But I'll giggle along on this bumbling trip.

So onward I go with a grin and a skip,
Chasing horizons, can't let laughter slip.
Each fork in the road brings a whimsical tease,
As I skip past the trees, just trying to please!

The Art of Becoming Whole

I'm a jigsaw puzzle missing some pieces,
Putting them together, my humor increases.
With a cat in my lap and crumbs on my shirt,
My life feels like one big comedy flirt.

Leaning on laughter like it's a crutch,
Finding joy in the chaos with just a touch.
I dance with odd bits, a kaleidoscope heart,
Fumbling my way, oh what a fine art!

A dash of love and a sprinkle of sass,
I'm baking this life in a mismatched glass.
Each laugh is a layer, each trip a new fold,
Mixing up stories in pots that are bold.

So here's to the blender that whirls with good cheer,
Creating a smoothie that's oddly unclear.
Yet I sip with a grin, all the flavors I'll fold,
For the art of becoming is humor untold!

Reflections in a Shattered Mirror

I glance in the shards that scatter my face,
Each crack holds a giggle, each line has a grace.
Who's that silly person, framed in this mess?
A jester in life, but who needs to impress?

I see my reflection wink back at me,
With mismatched socks and a hairstyle so free.
The stories it tells, through laughter and tears,
I'm the king of my castle, reigning in cheers!

This mirror won't show me a polished façade,
Just the real, hilarious truth that I laud.
Every chip in the glass makes me who I am,
A quirky adventure with laughter as jam.

So here's to the cracks, the quirks, and the shine,
In every reflection, there's joy intertwined.
Embrace every fragment, let laughter unfurl,
For we're all just a bit wild in this beautiful whirl!

www.ingramcontent.com/pod-product-compliance
Lightning Source LLC
Chambersburg PA
CBHW051645160426
43209CB00004B/793